THE MAN WITHIN ME: MY VICTORY
OVER PROSTATE CANCER

By Eric E. Ludin, Esq.

Foreword by Dr. Li-Ming Su, M.D.

ISBN-13: 978-1536894431

ISBN-10: 1536894435

First Printing, 2016

Printed in the USA by CreateSpace

The Man Within Me:

My Victory Over Prostate Cancer

By Eric E. Ludin, Esq.

Foreword by Dr. Li-Ming Su, M.D.

Don't be afraid of your fears. They're not there to scare you. They're there to let you know that something is worth it.

— C. JoyBell C.

Nothing in life is to be feared, it is only to be understood. Now is the time to understand more, so that we may fear less.

— Marie Curie

Thank you to my loving wife, Judy, who never once gave a moment of thought to how my situation would affect her life. She provided me with comfort and support throughout the entire process. For that I will be forever grateful.

2

Foreword

Be engaged, be educated, and be empowered. Having practiced urology since 2000 and specifically established a successful practice treating prostate cancer, I have had the unique opportunity to witness thousands of men and their partners present to my office with a new diagnosis of prostate cancer. I have been intrigued by the wide range of emotions and often dismayed at the utter confusion that patients have had regarding the contradicting information that they have received and ultimately the challenges that they face in seeking the right solution for their diagnosis.

This journey has become even more complex to navigate for patients as the myriad of treatment options for prostate cancer has seemingly increased by the year – not to mention the controversies of over-detection and over-treatment of certain prostate cancers – leaving some patients to wonder and regret having been tested for prostate cancer in the first place. Lastly, the unregulated nature of perhaps our most convenient resource, the Internet, has led to additional confusion as patients and their families rapidly search for the best doctors who quote the best statistics with the least amount of side effects, often not substantiated by a peer-reviewed process. In the end, patients need to avoid the trap of being mired in the "arms race" between surgery and radiation as well as their various forms. Instead, patients need to be better informed based on having an honest conversation that involves the following facts.

First, all men are not created equal and neither are their cancers. What I mean by this is that each patient presents a unique set of circumstances, including their age, medical conditions, life expectancy, pre-existing urinary and sexual function, presence of a sexual partner as well as stage (how extensive is the cancer) and grade (how aggressive is the cancer) of their prostate cancer. This means that each patient may respond better or worse to different treatments and they may experience a very different outcome than their well-meaning friend or family member who underwent prostate cancer treatment.

Second, treatment options (whether radiation or surgery) have improved significantly with better cure rates and less (but not absent of) side effects. Again, Uncle Bob's results and side effects from being treated a decade ago may look very different in this current era of high-tech medical care.

Third, there is no such thing as a perfect treatment for prostate cancer. Although treatment has improved significantly over the past three decades, both radiation and surgery are still associated with some degree of side effects and these side effects can impact a patient's (and often the partner's) quality of life. More importantly, the side-effect profile is different and can be more or less challenging for different patients based upon the patient's age, health, type of treatment, time since treatment, and other factors.

Fourth, there is not always one right answer as there is a current paucity of evidence for the "best" treatment between active surveillance, radiation, or surgery – especially when treating low-risk prostate cancer. There are risks and benefits to each of these options and the intelligent consumer must weigh these options carefully based upon a clear understanding of attendant complications and willingness to be subjected to the same. Finally, a patient needs to be aware that his vote counts. A patient's fundamental understanding that he has a choice in this decision is paramount. Furthermore, his philosophy about health, quality of life, and well-being factors significantly into making a sound choice of treatment.

In the end, the responsibility of the patient's many physicians are to provide transparent and factual information based upon the best current medical evidence to better prepare both the patient and partner for the many challenges that lie ahead whether active surveillance, radiation, or surgery is selected. Hand in hand with proper physician counsel is the unique experience from the patient's perspective. The emotional rollercoaster in selecting and then riding out the aftermath of treatment is unique to each individual. However, there is no doubt that there are common themes that all men ponder and fear in this process that cannot always be captured by his physician. The following book highlights one patient's journey from diagnosis to treatment and ultimately to recovery from a physical, psychosocial, and functional standpoint. It should be emphasized that this is only one man's perspective, but a perspective that will likely leave the reader engaged, perhaps laughing (or crying) at times, but certainly wiser than before the moment they open this book. – *Dr. Li-Ming Su, M.D.*

2016

TABLE OF CONTENTS

Introduction

I began writing this book shortly after my surgery when it occurred to me that I had just experienced a major life event that many men fear. I was diagnosed with prostate cancer at age 55 and had my prostate surgically removed at age 56. I had never written a book before, but took on the challenge because I felt that I had something to offer other men diagnosed with prostate cancer, other cancer, or serious illness.

I hope that this book will educate men interested in learning about what their experience might be. If you are reading this and have been diagnosed with prostate cancer, I hope that this book will answer questions you have about surgery and your life post-surgery. I hope it reduces the fear you may have about your diagnosis and treatment. I hope it helps provide you with the confidence you need to take the next step in treating your illness.

When I started writing, I made up my mind that I would not hold back any details because they are embarrassing or too private. I chose to share the most personal aspects of my disease, treatment, and recovery so that you will have a better understanding of what you might expect for your own experience. I seriously doubt there is anything written about prostate cancer with as much personal detail as you will read in this book. In fact, before publishing this, I had doctors read the book for accuracy and for their input. I was surprised to hear one doctor tell me that he learned quite a bit from my experience that he did not know regarding outcomes from surgery. In that regard, I hope that by sharing so much personal information, I am, to some modest extent, making a contribution to medicine. I have to thank my wonderful wife, Judy, for allowing me to share such intimate details about our private life. We both understand that it benefits others to know.

This book is short. I intended to make this an easy and quick read so that people who are not accustomed to lengthy books would not be intimidated. Much is written on cancer which cannot be understood by a person who has no formal medical training or who lacks a graduate degree. I wanted this book to be read and understood by anyone regardless of their educational background. The book does no one any good if it is not read and understood.

I am very mindful of the fact that I entered this process with advantages that you might not have. For instance, I am a partner in a law firm and had no fear of losing my job by taking time off for surgery. I had great health insurance accepted by my doctors and the hospital where my surgery took place. I had the financial resources to pay my deductible and co-pays. In the book, I talk about the advantages of joining a gym and hiring a personal trainer. Of course, most people do not have the extra cash to pay for that luxury. Probably the most significant and important resource I had, which made a huge difference in my treatment and recovery, was an understanding and supportive wife and family. I cannot overstate the importance of a support system when dealing with disease. I am truly blessed in that respect.

There is no doubt that my experience as described in this book will be different from your experience. Your disease will be at a different stage and be more or less aggressive. Your age and health will differ. Other factors will be considerably different such as your job, your geographic, financial access to good health care, and your family support system. But regardless of these differences, I encourage you not to be discouraged.

My treatment decision was not limited because of financial or geographic considerations. Your treatment choice may be limited in that way. However, as long as the treatment you select is one reasonably recommended by your physician, it is likely not a bad option and you should not feel that you have to compromise your health.

If you do not have a close family member or friend to confide in who would help you make your decision, there are support groups or other patients of your doctor who might be willing to talk to you and help. I asked my doctor for the name of a patient my age who made the decision to have surgery. After getting his consent, my doctor provided me with the patient's contact information. It helped me a great deal to speak to him. I encourage you to do the same.

I recently learned about an organization called The Reluctant Brotherhood which is a free telephone support group for people living with prostate cancer. Their website is www.thereluctantbrotherhood.org. If you need information from other men who are living with or survived prostate cancer, this organization is a fantastic resource. In addition, the participants in The Reluctant Brotherhood provide emotional support to one another. The organization was founded about six years ago by John Teisberg of St. Paul, Minnesota. John is a prostate cancer survivor who had prostate surgery to remove his tumor. He felt that his wife at the time was not capable of providing the emotional support that he needed. Finding it challenging to seek out help elsewhere, he formed this wonderful affinity group.

As we all know, men often have a very difficult time dealing with emotional upheaval. Daphne Rose Kingma, author of *The Men We Never Knew*, has said:

"We've dismissed men as the feelingless gender—we've given up on them. Because of the way boys are socialized, their ability to deal with emotions has been systematically undermined. Men are taught, point-by-point, not to feel, not to cry, and not to find words to express themselves."

However, simply because men may not be good at expressing their emotions does not mean they have none. Many women are simply not used to helping their husbands deal with their feelings. This relationship problem can become worsened when the man expresses his repressed feelings of fear and sadness through anger and pride. The Reluctant Brotherhood hosts bi-monthly telephone conference calls during which men from throughout the world can talk about these emotions with others going through, or having gone through, the same experience. One cannot overstate the emotional upheaval caused by a treatment that will often effect the functioning of the most masculine organ. Nor can one overstate the importance of dealing with these emotions in a healthy and safe manner.

There are two primary messages I wish to convey with this book. First: if you are diagnosed with prostate cancer, do not fear the treatment. While not pleasant, you will survive and continue to enjoy life at least as much as you ever had before. Second: I implore you to educate yourself about your options notwithstanding any economic, geographic, and family limitations you have. Make a decision. Get treatment. Make yourself healthy. What you do now will be your story.

Chapter One

The Luckiest Man on the Planet

If you have been fortunate enough to be diagnosed with early stage prostate cancer, count your blessings. Today, you are the luckiest man on the planet. Make a rational decision about what you will do about your diagnosis. Do it and never look back. Your family will love and respect you for it. You will set an example for your children about how to deal with life's adversities. The doctor will remove your cancer. No one will ever be able to remove the pride that you will have for the rest of your long life for the decision that you made.

Since being diagnosed with prostate cancer at the age of 55 and having my prostate removed, I have made myself available to speak with men diagnosed with prostate cancer with questions about my experience. I found many people I speak with are depressed about the diagnosis and what treatment will mean to their enjoyment of life. People are warned that if they treat the disease, they will suffer from impotence and incontinence, either temporarily or permanently to some degree, regardless of the treatment they select.

I was struck by how the potential for impotence and life with incontinence can severely impact most men psychologically. The fear of suffering either of these often freezes men into inaction. They would rather put off treatment than suffer such a loss. Sadly, inaction can lead to what was once a treatable disease turning into an unsolvable nightmare. Slowly, tumors grow and multiply. A small tumor located near the edge of the prostate which could easily be treated one year, may develop into a larger tumor protruding through the membrane of the prostate the following year. Nerves that could have been spared one day, must be removed the next. Cancerous cells once contained, may now be spreading throughout the body.

I often find myself reminding other men how blessed they are to live in a time when cancer in the prostate can be discovered so early. How they can take action to avoid a most painful and unpleasant death and go on to live a happy and fulfilling life for many more years.

As I see it, there are three main reasons not to take the recommended steps in response to a diagnosis of prostate cancer. The first is fear. Fear of the treatment, fear of a bad outcome, and fear of the unknown. As someone who has experienced the procedure, I can tell you that the fear of disease should be far greater than the fear of the treatment. The discomfort and pain of surgery is not that great. I rate this reason for ignoring treatment options as *illegitimate.*

The second reason not to treat is uncertainty about the proper course of action. This rationale is somewhat more sensible than being frozen by fear, but only slightly more sensible. Depending upon your diagnosis, you may be given a variety of options with no concrete recommendation from your physician to select one over the other. This places a burden on you as the patient to do research and make up your own mind as to which option is best for you. But, while uncertainty can delay a decision, it should not cause you to be frozen into inaction. Set a deadline and decide by the deadline. Once you decide, do not look back. If the decision you make is to go with a treatment option offered by your physician, you can feel comfortable in knowing that there is a rational medical reason to do what you are doing. You did not make the wrong decision.

The only legitimate reason I know of not to act upon a prostate cancer diagnoses is if you are a Christian Scientist. I know a Christian Scientist whose faith caused her to choose not to get medical treatment for cancer. This person acted with such grace and courage while the disease ravaged her body and destroyed her appearance. I greatly respected her decision because it was grounded in a strong religious belief. Her unwavering commitment to her faith was a positive inspiration for all who knew what she was battling. Her act not to treat was the polar opposite of fear and indecision. Although I do not subscribe to her beliefs, I gained tremendous respect for this valiant devout soul. Few people can live life with such a commitment.

When you consider your treatment options, remember that how you handle this important decision will be your legacy to your children and loved ones. Ask yourself if you want people to remember you as fearful and indecisive, or as someone who took control of a potentially deadly disease and moved on, after treatment or surgery, to enjoy life.

What is it like to die of prostate cancer? Of course we all die. Hopefully, we die peacefully and in our sleep. But with prostate cancer, it can metastasize to the lungs and other organs such as the bones. The sufferer may need oxygen and morphine. Lung metastasis is less common but can occur in very advanced stages. Bone metastasis is more common than lung metastasis, resulting in pain, pathologic fracture, and potential paralysis if the spinal cord is injured. Also, patients can have urinary obstruction and blood in their urine if the tumor grows and blocks their urinary channel, i.e. urethra. Thankfully, organizations like hospice will make the patient comfortable until their ultimate death to avoid too much suffering. From everything I read, dying from prostate cancer is not a good way to die.

When considering the side effects of treatment for prostate cancer, never forget that the fight is more to save your life than it is to save your erection. Even healthy men will lose their erection or interest in sex by a certain age. But, they continue to enjoy life. Healthy men and women may lose their ability to fully control their urine flow as they age, but they buy pads to wear in their underwear and continue to enjoy life. There is no reason to put your life at risk to prevent something from happening, which may happen anyway with time. As I have matured, I have come to realize that a man is judged not so much by how well he performs in bed, but by the strength of his character. There is not much that is sexier to a woman than a man who can decisively make difficult and brave decisions. If she is so attracted to you that she wants to have sex, and you have difficulty with that, there are other ways to please a woman sexually than by use of a strong penile erection. You can still be king of the bedroom.

Chapter Two

PSA

On my 50th birthday I began noticing that I was no longer a young man. It struck me that I was at least 10 years older than anyone else in my law firm. I was often the oldest person in a room. I would catch myself looking around airport lobbies and restaurant dining rooms to see if anyone was older than me.

Physically, I noticed subtle changes. What remained of my hair turned gray. By 53, I shaved it all off. I decided I would rather be completely bald than show one sliver of gray hair. Shaving my head was actually a terrific move to bolster my self-confidence. In my fantasy world, I imagine women of all ages finding my baldness sexy. Baldness made me feel that I was no longer a middle-aged man, but a young male virile brute who knows what he wants and knows how to get it and doesn't care what other people think. Nothing is sexier than a confident bald man!

Of course, the young women admiring me did not need to know that every morning I took cholesterol and blood pressure medication, Prilosec to help me cope with indigestion, and 20 mg of Cialis every Friday. If I held my gut in, they might not even notice the extra 10 pounds I carry around (OK... 15 lbs.). Pretty sexy, huh??

On this particular day, midway through my 55th year, I found myself sitting in a urologist's office. It seemed odd to me that I was easily the youngest patient sitting in the busy waiting room. I was dressed business casual, having come from my office, and felt out of place. I suspect the receptionist thought I was a salesman when I first walked up to her. The closest to my age was a man sitting in front of the TV who was at least 25 years my senior. He did not use a walker, but judging from his gait returning from the bathroom, he would have benefited from one. There were two other men in wheelchairs accompanied by a caregiver.

I had never seen a urologist before and did not know what to think when handed a cup upon arrival. I was directed to a wall with three bathroom doors which opened into the lobby. Upon entering, I noticed that the restroom was used all day and, judging from the trash can overflowing with paper towels; they must be visited by every patient who visits the clinic. On the wall, there was a shelf that turns on a lazy Susan with instructions to fill your cup, place it on the shelf, and spin it so that the staff can remove your urine on the other side of the wall. I wondered what my urine had to do with the reason for my visit. Clearly, a donation of urine was a precondition before seeing the doctor... along with the co-pay.

Returning to the waiting room, I noticed an older woman entering the office. I pulled out my smart phone and was about to ask Google why a woman would be seeing a urologist (what

26

is a urologist anyway?), when my name was called. I was about to see a urologist for the first time in my life.

How did I get here? Ever since I began taking pills for high cholesterol, I was getting blood drawn every six months to test my liver function. I understand that the medicine I take for cholesterol can affect my liver which must be monitored regularly. These semi-annual visits with my doctor meant regular monitoring and gave me confidence that serious health problems would not go unnoticed for long. Additionally, I began to develop a close relationship with my doctor who got to know me through these regular visits. As much as I would not choose to have high cholesterol, it probably was beneficial to my overall health – it obligated me to see my doctor often.

In preparation for my annual physicals every other visit, my general doctor had been ordering a Prostate-specific antigen, or PSA test. PSA is a protein produced by the cells of the prostate gland. A PSA test measures the amount of this protein in the blood. He started ordering the PSA on my 50th birthday. The PSA test did not cost me anything, nor did it require anything more of me. After all, my blood was being drawn to test liver function and for a myriad of other reasons.

Also, by the time I turned 50, my visits to my general doctor started to get a lot more personal. He directed me to drop my drawers, turn toward the exam table, and bend over. The rectal exam is emotionally challenging for a lot of men. To this day, I am shocked at how many men tell me they refuse to allow their doctor to give them a rectal prostate exam. It is not so much painful as it is unpleasant. For a few moments, men must give up control and allow themselves to be penetrated in an anatomical location not normally penetrated. There is absolutely no reason to refuse to allow the test. It may be uncomfortable for a moment, but it causes no lasting harm to a typical, well-adjusted man. Until my fifth test, these PSA results and digital exams were always normal.

Up until a week prior to my first visit to the urologist, I did not know much about the prostate. I understood that it was a male body part that would frequently become enlarged and make urination difficult as had happened to my father. It could also often become cancerous. I also knew that prostate cancer develops very slowly. As far as I knew, no member of my family had ever had prostate cancer, except for my father-in-law. He developed prostate cancer in his 80s and had radiation therapy. He was never too concerned about his prostate cancer having been assured that he would die of some other cause. In fact, he did die of other causes at age 92. Other than knowing that this male body part could become cancerous, I had no idea what the prostate's function was. I would soon learn.

I received a phone call from my doctor's office. They had received my blood-test results in advance of my regular annual physical and the nurse wanted me to know that my PSA was elevated. She was passing along a message from the doctor that he wanted me to see a urologist. In her calm voice, the nurse told me not to be too concerned. She advised that my PSA was 4.1 (on whatever scale they use). She said that 4.0 or less was considered to be normal. I asked why the doctor felt alarmed enough to refer me to a specialist when it was so close to normal. She said that he was more concerned about the change in the PSA from the previous year. One year earlier, my PSA was 1.4 and such an increase in 12 months was uncommon and somewhat disconcerting.

I did as I was told and scheduled the appointment. However, I am curious by nature, so I was compelled to do some personal research about elevated PSAs. What I learned caused me to be confident that I was wasting my time visiting a urologist. I went to Google seeking to find out the various causes of elevated PSAs. I read that a PSA can be elevated by numerous factors not related to cancer. For instance, riding a bicycle or having sex can temporarily elevate your PSA. It turns out that the prostate is located in a region between a man's testicles and rectum. This is the very same area that can be irritated by a bicycle seat.

My wife and I had recently moved to downtown St. Petersburg, Florida. We previously lived in the suburbs and rarely had reason to ride our bicycles. But, living downtown, we rode almost daily. To me, my bike riding represented a convenient explanation for why my PSA would change over the prior year. It made perfect sense.

I am not sure when I had sex prior to my PSA test. But, if sex could cause an elevated PSA that provided yet another possible cause for the abnormal test result. I learned that the primary purpose of the prostate is to generate and mix semen with sperm to create the male ejaculate. It made sense to me as a layman that having an ejaculation stimulates the prostate and can cause an elevation of the PSA. If riding my bicycle and having sex caused elevated PSA and if I were just above normal levels, visiting a urologist because of the PSA seemed like a ridiculous waste of time.

My paralegal's husband had seen the same urologist that I was visiting. She told me that the doctor was very good, but had a less than excellent demeanor. He gave her the sad news that her husband had bladder cancer and did not deliver the news well. I was not particularly concerned about getting bad news nor was his bedside manner a consideration. I was meeting him because I was told to and fully expected it to be very brief.

As I waited for the doctor to enter the exam room, I looked at the tools of his trade situated around the room. I started to panic when I remembered what others had told me about things a urologist will often do. I recalled hearing stories of doctors shoving tubes in the penis and how ridiculously painful it was. Was I about to have a tube inserted inside my penis to examine my prostate? I started to think that showing up for this appointment would soon prove to be an agonizing mistake. A nurse entered the room to take my blood pressure and ask me a few questions. I could not wait to ask her mine. She assured me that nothing would be thrust into my penis and my blood pressure returned to normal. I suppose that if I had known what the doctor had planned for me, I might not have been so calm.

As the doctor entered the exam room, I knew within moments that I would like him. I also understood why others might not warm up to him. He spoke with a heavy accent and I later learned that he had attended medical school in China. He had a sense of humor that was likely lost on some of his senior citizen patients. As he started to speak, he stopped sharply in mid-sentence and pointed to my law firm logo on my shirt. "What is that?" he asked. When I told him that I was a lawyer and that was my logo, I quickly followed it up with the comment, "and we do not sue doctors." He laughed enthusiastically and I understood that he had a quick wit and we would get along just fine. He turned out to have a fun and odd sense of humor which greatly helped to relieve my stress during the next visit.

After the digital prostate exam which appeared normal, we got down to business. The doctor explained to me that my elevated PSA was not normal because of the significant increase over the prior year's test and he recommended that I have a biopsy of the prostate. He attempted to alleviate my concerns by telling me that there was an 80% chance that I did not have cancer and, even if I did, it would likely be very treatable. At that moment, I smirked. He had just told me that I had a 20% chance of having cancer. I did not believe him. There was no way that I had cancer and felt he was simply looking to do a procedure. My PSA was nearly normal and who ever heard of someone so young being diagnosed with prostate cancer? Isn't prostate cancer a disease that only effects people in their 70s and 80s? So I decided to use my legal skills and cross exam this doctor. Surely within minutes, he would admit that the biopsy was unnecessary.

Me: *If there is an 80% chance that my elevated PSA is not caused by cancer, what other causes could there be*?

Doctor: *It could be infection in prostate. This often cause of elevated PSA.* (add Asian accent)

Me: *Could bike riding or sex also cause an elevated PSA?*

Doctor: *Yes.*

Me: *Isn't it rare for prostate cancer to be diagnosed in someone in their 50s?*

Doctor: *It is unusual, but happens.*

A trial lawyer knows not to ask any question without knowing the answer. But, I proceeded anyway with the one question that would certainly win the argument for me. I was convinced that I was about to walk out with no tests ordered.

Me: *So, rather than doing a biopsy, wouldn't it make more sense to prescribe an antibiotic then retake the PSA and, of course, go without bike riding or sex for a few days prior?*

I did not expect what happened next. He asked me a rhetorical question which sealed the deal and killed my argument.

Doctor: *So, let me ask you question. If you do what you say, and your PSA goes from 4.1 to 3.5, would you conclude that you do not have cancer?*

His question stopped me in my tracks. He followed his question up with a counter-punch which I later realized were a set of white lies.

Doctor: *I recommend you have biopsy. If you do, you will know whether you have cancer or not. It is quick and easy test. Just do it.*

He actually said two white lies. One was that he inferred that the biopsy will be conclusive as to whether I have cancer. The truth is that you can find cancer in a biopsy, but you cannot rule it out if you do not find cancer. Sometimes the cancerous tumor can be missed by the needle biopsy. The second white lie was that the test was quick and easy. Actually, it was quick and likely easy for him. For me, it took the digital rectal exam's discomfort to a whole new level.

In retrospect, I consider my urologist to be a hero. He may have saved my life. If he had not so strongly directed me toward the biopsy, I would likely have not had it done in the interest of conservative medical care.

When I got in the car, I called my wife Judy and told her about the appointment. I told her that she should not be concerned because I had an

80 percent chance of not having cancer. She said what was on my mind, but I refused to say out loud. "I don't like those odds." Until I went to see the doctor, we did not believe that a cancer diagnosis was a potential reality. We had thought the referral to a urologist was just an example of a doctor being overly cautious. Now we realized that an elevated PSA was serious. My PSA earned me a ticket to a urologist. No, I was no longer a young man with a healthy prostate. I had visited the specialist for good reason and would no longer feel so out of place in the lobby of his office sitting with all the seniors.

I reassured Judy that all would be OK, that I did not have cancer and even if I did, they could easily treat it. She agreed that it would be better to be safe than sorry, and I told her about my biopsy scheduled for later in the week.

Chapter Three

Biopsy

The prostate is located adjacent and in close proximity to the rectum. Apparently the easiest and most common way to access the prostate for a biopsy is by using a needle inserted through the wall of the rectum. To avoid an infection of the prostate, I was instructed to take an antibiotic before the procedure as well as a fleet enema. My butt was going to be violated and I was not looking forward to it.

I will preface this story by pointing out that a prostate biopsy may not be fun, but it is not something that should be dreaded. It is not as painful as many of my dental cleanings or any more uncomfortable. Given a choice between a root canal and a prostate biopsy, I'd take the biopsy every time. Of course I would prefer to have neither, but remember that the root canal alleviates pain and the biopsy can save your life.

The bottom line is, do not allow fear of the procedure to stop you from getting the test. It is not that bad. We routinely experience more pain when we have other procedures.

When I arrived at the urologist's office for the biopsy, I was again asked for a urine sample though I still have no clue why. A young female nurse had me remove my pants and lay on my side on the exam table. It was about to become a memorably awkward day. When the doc entered the room he explained that he would be inserting an ultrasound device into my rectum. It would help the physician see the prostate and guide his needle which ran alongside the ultrasound unit. He explained that he would take 12 tissue core samples from various parts of the prostate.

Each time he took a sample, it felt like the needle was fired into the prostate. Each sample was taken quickly followed by moments of searching for the next target sight. I was not comfortable in this position with a tube up my rear, so I decided to relieve my stress through humor. I told the doctor that the prior night I had a nightmare that a man stuck a large object in my rear. We both had a good laugh and, before I knew it, he was done. The entire biopsy procedure lasted a half hour.

I have since learned that you can have this biopsy done under anesthesia. I am glad that I did not do it that way. With this method, I was able to immediately return to work. I suspect that if I needed to have this done annually, I might consider using anesthesia. But, fortunately, that decision became moot.

Before leaving, I scheduled my next appointment to return for the results. The doctor assured me that I likely did not have cancer and, even if I did, it would be treatable. He told me not to worry or lose sleep. I would not and did not. I was certain it was not cancer and was relieved that this experience was behind me.

Probably the most disturbing part of the biopsy is the bleeding that follows. The nurse had me put gauze between my butt cheeks so that blood from my rectum would not get on my underwear. I only needed to have the gauze for a few hours. But, the bleeding is not over. The biopsy needle not only cuts through the rectum, but it also punctures the urethra. This means that you will have blood from your rectum, in your urine, and in your semen.

I cannot imagine how frightened I would have been had the nurse not warned me about the blood. While the rectal bleeding was minor and short lived, it took weeks before my urine was clear and months before it was out of my semen. Although I expected my semen to be red, it actually looked to me like my penis was shooting blood. I bought a box of condoms to use until it cleared.

I do not recall any residual pain from the procedure. I went back to my office to work immediately after it was over.

The following week, I returned to the urologist's office. For the first time in three visits, I did not need to donate urine to the staff behind the lazy Susan. I was escorted back to the same exam room I was in for the prior two visits and waited for the doctor to give me the news. Regardless of the results, I was not worried. I figured the worst case scenario was that I had cancer and they had caught it early. From what I read, prostate cancer develops very slowly. This gave me more reason not to worry.

The moment he entered the room, I knew the answer. Not because he told me. But because of the prickly way he looked at me and his first words, "How was recovery from biopsy?" I answered him quickly knowing that he was just stalling before telling me the real news. I knew that if the tests were negative, those would have been the first words out of his mouth. I told him I was fine.

"Well, I have bad news for you," he said. "You do have cancer."

I was jolted. Although I tried to prepare myself for the worst, I really don't know that anyone is ever prepared to hear those words. He told me that of the 12 core samples he took, 11 were clear and one showed cancer. He said that this was not unusual since finding cancer in the prostate can be like trying to grab a seed from a strawberry. They can be so small that even 12 core samples might miss a cancerous tumor entirely. In fact, there was a good chance that I have more than one tumor in the prostate.

He told me that I had a Gleason score 6. A what? I had never heard this term before and was about to learn about a lot of things I never knew before. The Gleason score, he explained, is a system of grading prostate cancer tissue based on how it looks under a microscope. It is a predictor for how aggressive your cancer cells are and how likely it may spread. The Gleason pattern ranges from 1-5 and the value of the two most representative patterns of cancer that are seen in the prostate biopsy tissues are added, arriving at a sum score, i.e. 3+3=6. The Gleason scores range from a low of 2 to a high of 10. He said that my score was not low, but it did indicate that the cancer has likely not spread and that I did catch it early.

He then clarified that my cancer was very treatable and I should not be concerned. Terrific, I thought. I figured that this meant that I could take a pill or have some kind of therapy to kill the cancer. His next comment floored me.

"I want you to see a surgeon in Gainesville", he said. "He is outstanding and we are very fortunate to have him in our state. His name is Dr. Li-Ming Su." "What type of surgery would he do?" I asked, figuring that he could remove the tumor from my prostate. "He will remove the prostate," he responded.

I was shocked. Remove my prostate? What happened to treatment? He told me bluntly that it was the best option for me. I could choose to do nothing and have annual biopsies

and hope the cancer does not spread, or else I
could choose to have surgery. He said that he
did not think that I would be a good candidate
for the surveillance approach since he figured
my personality would not allow me to live with
cancer. He said that radiation was not a good
option for someone my age (55) since the
treatment might not last for my entire life span.

I asked him how this surgery would impact my
life. He hurriedly told me that I would lose
continence for a while. I imagined what it would
be like to argue a case in the courtroom wearing
a diaper and smelling of urine. He also told me
that I would lose my ability to have an erection
but quickly added that this function might
return with time. He said that I may have to
start using Cialis or Viagra. When I told him that
I already did, he frowned and said that this does
not bode well. "Usually people who use them
prior to prostate surgery have a more difficult
time with potency," he explained. He said that
there are other ways to treat impotency and

that I should deal with the cancer first. Again, he told me to see Dr. Su and sent me on my way out the door.

As I walked back to my car, I had a better understanding for why people were not crazy about this doctor's blunt bedside manner. I pondered the possibility of becoming impotent and incontinent as I drove back to the office. I felt perfectly healthy. I considered myself to be young and active. There was no way I was about to give up my sex life for what seemed like an overly aggressive approach to catching cancer very early. I was not going to go to court and pee in my pants while arguing to a jury. At that moment, I believed that the urologist was being an alarmist. With a slow growing cancer, I need not change my lifestyle at such a young age. I had years before I would even consider surgery.

I called my wife and we agreed that I would see the doctor in Gainesville. But, it would merely be part of a fact finding mission. I was sure at the time that I would prefer the conservative, wait and see approach. Later, I could choose an option that could stop the cancer and allow me to continue living my normal life. I figured that, if the surgeon was as excellent as promised, he would agree. This was not an emergency and I was not about to make a decision that would alter the quality and enjoyment of my life.

Looking back today, I am forever grateful to my urologist. He insisted I have a biopsy when I believed it was not necessary. He skillfully located cancerous tissue which could easily have been missed. Most importantly, he referred me to an outstanding physician who provided the advice and guidance I needed and ultimately performed the surgery I chose to have. Because of what this urologist did for me, I feel as though I dodged a bullet. I am a very fortunate person to have been treated by this man.

Chapter Four

Surgeon

After calling my wife, I spoke to my mother and my children. I was not panicked or worried and they responded in the same manner. We all knew of people who had prostate cancer and died of other causes. We reassured each other that since this was caught early, I would be fine. I do not know if everyone in the family really shared my confidence or just put up a good front to support me emotionally. But regardless, I felt calm and accepted the urologist's recommendation to see a surgeon. I scheduled an appointment to see Dr. Su at University of Florida Health Shands Hospital.

I Googled Dr. Su and learned that he is the chief of the Division of Robotic and Minimally Invasive Urologic Surgery at the UF, who conducts hundreds of procedures using the da Vinci Robotic Surgical System. He trained at

Johns Hopkins University Hospital in Baltimore and had been at UF for about six years.

I only live about 2½ hours from Gainesville and drove up the morning of the appointment. My wife and I had lunch with my son, a student at UF. On a corner of the UF campus was the UF Health Medical Plaza. The urology department was on the third floor. After lunch with my son, we checked in at the Medical Plaza. I was quickly called to the exam room where I met a very young Asian man. He did not look old enough to be a doctor, let alone one with years of experience. It turned out he was not Dr. Su. This youngster introduced himself as a recent medical school graduate training in the hospital's residency program. As a teaching hospital, I would meet many residents while there. He went through my history and we briefly discussed the Gleason score. I submitted to the obligatory digital prostate exam. Thankfully, he had very thin fingers. After we spoke for about 15 minutes, he left the room telling me that Dr. Su would be here shortly.

Dr. Su entered not long after. He appeared to be in his mid-forties. He was relaxed and had a pleasant demeanor. He treated me with warmth and a caring attitude. I later learned that this was a side of him reserved for the patients. Those who work with him see a man who has a type A personality, is a perfectionist, and is very demanding. He keeps everyone who works with him on their toes, lacks tolerance for sloppiness, and does not suffer fools.

Dr. Su spoke with me for at least an hour, and only left when he was sure that I ran out of questions. Before explaining my options, he asked me many detailed personal questions. Among other things, he wanted to know about my sex life and how my potency compared to what it was when I was 18. He asked about my frequency of urination and whether I ever had difficulties. He explained that no matter what treatment option I selected, it would affect my urinary continence and sexual potency. Using a whiteboard, he wrote out my options based on my Gleason score and age. All were medically reasonable options and only I could decide which to select. Even though he was a surgeon, he never encouraged surgery over other options.

He explained that I had three options. The first was "active surveillance." This selection basically meant that I would do nothing to treat the cancer. But, every year I would have a PSA test and prostate biopsy. The decision to treat would be delayed indefinitely until something changed. He said that this was an acceptable option because prostate cancer grows slowly and might never spread. But, he said that this was only true for me because of my low volume, low Gleason score tumor (i.e. 1 core positive for Gleason 6 cancer). For other patients, this would not be a viable option.

I was unhappy to learn that active surveillance required annual biopsies. I could not see myself dealing with that on a regular basis followed by the bleeding. I wondered how many biopsies I could put myself through before caving in to treatment. Plus, wasn't active surveillance just putting off the inevitable? Wouldn't the cancer grow eventually? Also, how much trauma could a prostate take? Could it really handle being needled once a year for the rest of my life? I ruled this out completely when Dr. Su told me that a prostate that has been biopsied numerous times is often more difficult to remove surgically because of the scar tissue damage. Before I arrived for the appointment, surveillance was the only option I intended to pursue. But, because of the annual biopsies, it was no longer a choice I would consider. Before we left the appointment, I was convinced that this was not an option for me.

The two remaining options available to me were radiation and surgery. Understand that these are not necessarily the only remaining treatment options available. But, these were the only two that Dr. Su said would be appropriate for me to consider given my age, Gleason score, and physical condition. He spent a great deal of time explaining the ramifications of each choice. We talked about the treatment, recovery, and short- and long-term effects. Both would result in changes in my ability to hold urine and get an erection.

With surgery, I would no longer be able to have an ejaculation with sex. But, he assured me that I could still have an orgasm though it would be "dry." He explained that the orgasm originates in the brain. The ejaculation occurs simultaneously with the orgasm. But, you do not need an ejaculation to have an orgasm. He said that some people report that the dry orgasm is not as satisfying as a wet orgasm. I would later learn that this is not the case for me.

I asked why he needed to remove the entire prostate if I only had one tumor. He told me that partial removal of sections of a prostate is not an accepted way to treat prostate cancer. The biopsies often miss other tumors and there is no guarantee that the cancer cells have not spread throughout the prostate. If he operates, it all has to go.

He also explained that the nerves which permit one to be potent are located along the periphery of the prostate. He described these nerves as being attached to a material not dissimilar to the outer layer of an onion. Very thin and fragile. He said that he could not assure me that the nerves would be saved. He explained that he would excise a portion of the nerves if the tumor turned out to be in contact or close proximity to them. He advised that it is important not to leave cancer in the body in order to protect my potency.

I asked about the connection between the prostate and urinary continence. I learned that there are three major muscles that allow you to be continent. These consist of a sphincter type muscle at the base of the bladder, the prostate itself, and the muscles on the pelvic floor often referred to as the Kegel muscles. The Kegel muscles are those that a man uses to stop or interrupt his urinary flow. Men have all tried that when the phone rings while urinating. The surgery removes the bladder sphincter and prostate muscles leaving only those on the pelvic floor to control urine flow. This leaves the man in a position very similar to a woman's with regard to continence. Fortunately, these muscles are easier to train when you have surgery at a younger age. Regardless of my decision, I was resolved to start Kegel exercises immediately.

The final option was radiation. Radiation, he explained, involved going to a radiologist daily for 40-45 treatment sessions. One may also have radioactive seeds implanted. He said that radiation permanently affects the tissue in the prostate. Whereas you may not notice any significant change in potency at first, over time, your performance will decline. The patient's ability to urinate does not get effected immediately, but over time, it can be more difficult or painful to urinate. Frequency and urgency to urinate and defecate is common following radiation due to the effects on the bladder and colon. These changes caused by radiation can be permanent and difficult to treat.

I was disturbed to learn that there is not a great deal of research to indicate the long-term rate of recurrence of prostate cancer 15 years after treatment. Although radiation therapy is very effective, he warned me that there is no guarantee it would not return many years after the treatment. Since I was so young, I worried that this would not be a permanent cure. I asked if we could have radiation now and surgery if it came back. Dr. Su explained that once the tissue is altered through radiation, surgery is often not an option. I later learned that there are a handful of doctors in the world who will do surgery following radiation, but not many.

I asked about new treatment options on the horizon. Could I wait a few years and have more choices? Dr. Su assured me that I should not expect this and not to delay treatment hoping for a panacea right around the corner. He recommended that I buy and read Dr. Patrick Walsh's *Guide to Surviving Prostate Cancer*. Dr. Su trained with Dr. Walsh at Johns Hopkins. He is considered the prostate cancer guru and had written one of the best technical books on the subject for patients.

Dr. Su suggested I go home, read the book, consider my options carefully, and make a decision. He said that he would do my surgery if I decided to go that route. He said there was no emergency and I could schedule whenever I wanted. He added that if I chose surgery, I would be home for about 4 weeks recovering before I could return to work.

I mentioned that, if I had surgery, I would like to do it in January. Since it was September, I could enjoy the nice fall weather, travel, sail, and be laid up for January or February. My wife and I have a 35-foot sailboat. Each spring we sail from St. Petersburg to Key West, stopping at various anchorages along the way. I told Dr. Su that if I had the surgery in the winter, I would be recovered enough by the spring to enjoy our annual trip. "Don't forget," he said, "you will likely still be incontinent in the spring."

As we drove home from Gainesville, my wife and I reviewed all the options. We both marveled at how much we appreciated Dr. Su and how impressed we were. We both felt extremely confident that if we elected to have surgery, we could trust him to do it. We were astounded by how much time he gave us explaining the situation and options. He even gave me his e-mail address so that I could follow up if I had any questions.

We discussed what to do next. We ordered the book that Dr. Su recommended.

Driving up to Gainesville, I planned to approach this diagnosis conservatively and only have surgery as a last result. Driving home from Gainesville, I was leaning toward removing the prostate and preparing myself for surgery. I was not remotely interested in active surveillance. The one thing I knew was that I did not want to live with cancer in my body.

In addition to reading the recommended book, I promised myself that I would learn more about the radiation option. I have a close friend, Dr. Zucel Solc, a radiation oncologist. He had been out of town on vacation throughout this process and I had been unable to speak with him. Dr. Solc had treated my father-in-law with radiation pellets and was a close friend of the family and a highly respected physician. I scheduled an appointment to meet with him upon his return.

Chapter Five

Decision

On my drive up to Gainesville, I was certain that I would not be in a hurry for surgery. Driving home that same day, my mindset, with the direction of car, had done a 180-degree turnaround. I wanted to schedule the surgery soon. The cancer had to go.

As a general rule, I had always believed it best to treat health conditions conservatively. For instance, when I noticed my cholesterol edging up, I did not immediately start taking medication to control it. Instead, I began treatment by increasing my regular exercise and watching my diet until such time as I realized that alone was not effective. Only then did I start medication. I would never have elective surgery without first exhausting all other options. In fact, up to this point, I had never had surgery in my life. So, why the sudden change in attitude?

First, I found myself believing in Dr. Su. Even though he made no promises about the outcome of surgery, I felt extremely confident in his abilities to do the job. Second, I knew that I did not want to have cancer. Even if it were growing slowly, I did not want it in me. Third, I felt there was no better time than the present. As I continued to age, I believed that my ability to recover from surgery would become more challenging and less certain.

As these thoughts went through my mind, I realized that I owed it to myself to do the research and speak to my friend the radiation oncologist. Even though I sensed that I was setting up artificial hurdles to leap over before reaching my eventual conclusion, I knew that I would regret it if I took a shortcut to the finish line.

As soon as I got home, I ordered Dr. Walsh's book on prostate cancer and scheduled my appointment with Dr. Solc. I have known Dr. Zucel Solc and his lovely wife for decades. We knew him by his nickname, Zunya. He has a wonderful sense of humor and I cannot envision him without a smile on his face. Zunya was the physician who inserted radioactive seed implants on my father-in-law's prostate years earlier. He was well aware of all the recent developments in the field of radiation therapy. I am blessed to have him as a friend as well as a doctor.

Dr. Solc's office is beautiful. When I arrived, I saw that his staff goes out of its way to make the office inviting and comfortable. Many of the clinic's patients come daily for their treatment and help themselves to coffee and breakfast food in the lobby. If it were right for me, I can see showing up for weeks on end before work to have my radiation therapy.

I was led back to his exam room. Now, as I write this book, I simply cannot recall whether I submitted to a digital prostate exam. I suppose I did. But frankly, by this time it was getting to be routine and no longer memorable. If it happened, I quickly forgot about it. Thinking back on it now, I should have been getting worried about myself.

Zunya and I discussed the benefits of radiation over surgery. He told me that radiation is very effective now. With new treatment methods and technology, they could successfully target and kill the tumors using Intensity-modulated radiation therapy (IMRT). Although I had been warned that there was not research to support the effectiveness IMRT more than 15 years after therapy, Zunya did not seem so concerned. He explained that a reoccurrence of cancer after therapy is an extremely rare event in his experience. However, he had concerns about radiation treatment as it related to me.

I told him that I had been diagnosed with a mild case of ulcerative colitis. For years I had flare-ups of colitis that would usually dissipate quickly with mild drugs. Ulcerative colitis is a form of inflammatory bowel disease. Inflammatory bowel disease, not be confused with IBS (irritable bowel syndrome), is a condition with chronic or recurring immune response and inflammation of the gastrointestinal tract.

Dr. Solc explained that radiation can negatively affect organs located near the prostate, especially if they are already compromised. Since I had been diagnosed with ulcerative colitis, he felt that I would be susceptible to damage to the colon. There was risk that my mild case of IBD could become a very serious one. I later asked my gastroenterologist about this and he confirmed that he had seen many patients whose IBD became much worse after radiation treatment, sometimes requiring surgery to remove damaged sections of the digestive system. For this reason, Dr. Solc did not want to treat me with radiation. He felt that the risk of damage from the treatment was too great. In his mind, my options were limited to active surveillance or surgery.

Dr. Solc was also a bit concerned about whether my Gleason score 6 was correct. He noted that my PSA one year earlier was significantly lower than my current PSA. The PSA had increased so rapidly, from 1.4 to 4.1, that he wondered whether the cancer was more aggressive than a Gleason 6. He wrote me a prescription for another PSA, "just out of curiosity," he said. I could sense that he was a little concerned that my condition might need attention faster than originally thought.

As I walked out the door, Zunya told me that this time, I was to go at least 3 days before the test without riding my bike and without sex. "Also," he warned as pointed his index finger at me, "no masturbation during those 3 days either!"

As I read through Dr. Walsh's book, I learned nothing significantly different than what I had already been told by Dr. Solc and Dr. Su. The book both confirmed what Dr. Su told me about the lack of long-term studies involving the success of radiation. I concluded that radiation is a valid form of treatment for older men, less likely to recover easily from surgery, whose life expectancy suggested they would be much more susceptible to dying from causes other than a reoccurrence of prostate cancer. This did not influence my decision since I already knew that I would not get radiation therapy.

I did not need the book to tell me that I would not want to put off treatment and merely engage in active surveillance. There was no way I would have the biopsy annually just to wait for the time when I would learn the cancer had gotten worse. I was determined to treat this now and put it out of my life.

Dr. Walsh's book did give me an idea of what to expect from surgery. I read about the worst possible outcomes and the risk of impotence and incontinence. I learned about what to expect and the benefits to the various types of surgery. Although robotic surgery uses the most advanced equipment, it seemed clear that the best equipment does not necessarily alter the ultimate result, especially if it is in the wrong hands. The robotic equipment is only as good as the operator. I read that if you choose to have the surgery done robotically, make certain your surgeon has done the procedure at least 500 times before you. I wondered how anyone gets the experience if no one will let an inexperienced surgeon operate on them.

By the way, I later asked Dr. Su that question. He explained that residents and fellows in training learn how to use the da Vinci robot using a computer simulator. Once they can do surgery, they participate on simpler parts of the operation often under the watchful eye of the senior faculty member. After doing the simpler portions of the operation many times and becoming skillful and experienced with the instruments, they can move on to more difficult steps and procedures.

I learned that the primary advantage to a robotic procedure as opposed to open surgery or laparoscopic surgery is the recovery. Rarely does a robotically done procedure necessitate a blood transfusion. The patient can often be discharged the day after surgery rather than recover in the hospital for days or weeks. But, in terms of the actual outcome and the ability to spare nerves, one type of surgery has not been proven to be more effective than another.

As part of my research, I located two men, both my age, who had their prostate removed using robotic surgery. One of the men had it performed by Dr. Su. The other had it done by a physician in Philadelphia. Both men reported quick and easy recoveries and have continued to have an active sex life and are continent. Both men had wonderful attitudes and loved their surgeons. After hanging up the phone, my decision was made. The surgery was scheduled.

I did have my follow up PSA test done as requested by Dr. Solc. I strictly followed his instructions about sex, bike riding, and masturbation. I was shocked by the results. After having a biopsy which definitely showed the existence of cancer in the prostate, my PSA had returned to 1.4. Ostensibly, my bike riding and sex had caused my PSA to be temporarily elevated. This temporary status led me to have a prostate biopsy. The biopsy showed cancer and I would soon have the cancer removed. I still consider what might have happened had I not gotten this anomaly of a PSA. The cancer could have grown undetected for years. Eventually it would have been discovered. Perhaps it would have been discovered too late.

Chapter Six

Preparation

I made my decision to proceed with surgery in October and scheduled the surgery four months later. I decided to give myself time to prepare physically and emotionally. Even more importantly, I wanted to enjoy the great fall sailing in Florida and a family ski trip I had planned for December. Looking back on it now, I believe these four months were probably the best of my life.

Most sailboats work comfortably and optimally when there are 15 knots of wind and smooth seas. Of course, having the wind blow from a favorable direction makes a great day into a perfect day. The boat moves fast and smoothly cuts through the sea. Even if you hate boats or tend to get seasick, you would likely love to be there at that time. Almost anyone could appreciate the art of sailing when conditions are ideal. But, unfortunately, perfect conditions happen rarely.

In Florida, I can sail all year around. If I sailed 52 weekends each year, I could count on one hand the number of times conditions are ideal. To be a true sailor, you have to enjoy the less than optimal times. Most of the time, the wind is either too strong or too weak. I lost count of the number of trips when I found myself heading south into a strong blow from the south, only to return north after the wind shifted 180 degrees, again, right on the nose. But, notwithstanding Murphy's Law of wind direction, *if you want to head in a particular direction count on the wind coming from there*, I love to sail. Sailing is my passion.

When I am not working, I am often sailing. If I am not working and not sailing, I am likely working on my boat. Few activities teach as much about life as sailing. A sailor learns that most of what you deal with is completely out of your control. Sailing is learning how to adapt to what life presents. There is an ancient piece of sailing wisdom repeated so many times, yet attributed to too many different people to know who first said it. It is that you cannot control the direction of the wind, but you can adjust your sails. When the wind is too weak, adjust your time schedule and be patient. When the wind is too strong, reduce sail. When the wind is coming from the wrong direction, tack and change estimated time of arrival. When things break, fix them. When conditions are rough and the waves are crashing around you, and the boat is pounding and you are cold and wet and sick, know that at the end of the day (or the next), things will be calm again and you will be dry. But, no matter how unpleasant it is, you are blessed to be sailing. When things are really bad, you feel truly alive and privileged to be experiencing nature in ways that few people can.

Where I live in Florida, I am just a few blocks from the waterfront. I often ride my bike in the morning along Tampa Bay. Every time I do it, I see a lone city employee sitting on a bench overlooking the water. He goes there every morning before work. I see hundreds of people walking, jogging, meditating, and practicing yoga. The water draws people to it like a magnet. There is an instinctive bond between humans and water. It is said that 80% of the world's population lives within 60 miles of a body of water. But, notwithstanding this natural desire to live near the water, few leave the safety of land, to go boating. Why is this?

Of course, one reason might be expense. Boating is not a cheap hobby. But, if you really want to get out on the water, anyone can. There are a group of men who hang around my marina. They fish off a small metal rowboat. They fish and eat what they catch. They do not buy bait. Instead, they knock the mussels off the pilings, crack open the shell, and use the meat for bait. No one needs to go hungry if they live near the water.

I think the biggest reason why people do not venture onto the water is fear. Fear of allowing nature to take over control of your world. When there is wind and waves, you will be shaken very hard.

Of course, the truth is that people stay on land and look at the water because they feel safe. It is ironic though, that being on land is far more dangerous than being at sea. As I type this, I am cruising 5 miles off the coast of Florida. I just read an article on line that was in today's paper about a 22-year-old killed in his motorcycle by a hit and run driver. There were at least five tragic events reported in today's newspaper not one of which involved someone at sea. At this moment, there is not another human outside of my boat within 5 miles of me. Crime is the furthest concern from my mind. I feel that at this moment, there is no safer place in the world than the exact spot where this boat is located.

Many people have boats but never use them. Most of the boats in my marina stay tied up to their docks. Why do people pay slip fees for boats they never use? A boat broker told me that these boats represent dreams of sailing away. Their owners do not act on their dreams, but they cannot sell the boats either. Selling the boat represents giving up on their dream. But, untying the boat from the dock, leaving the shoreline, and heading out whatever the conditions, makes me truly happy. I want to live my dreams.

Some of my best sailing stories are about overcoming challenging situations that I did not plan or want. I am proudest of the jury rig I assembled to get me home when a critical boat part buckled. No one is interested in me telling them about the perfect sailing trip. But, surviving an unpredicted storm at sea makes for a great yarn and terrific memory. I did not want my boat to break and I did not want to get caught in a storm, and I certainly did not want to be diagnosed with prostate cancer, but pride of overcoming these challenges is immeasurable.

I once had the experience of sailing from Key West to Naples with my brother-in-law, Mark, as crew. Mark enjoyed sailing with me, but was fairly inexperienced himself. A friend traveled with us in his own boat on the same trip. He had two crew members with him who were also inexperienced. The trip would take us about 19 hours non-stop. We agreed to leave Key West at noon and planned to arrive in Naples at 7am the next day. We both had boats that were the same size and would travel near each other. We checked the weather forecast and saw that a storm would be passing through the next morning. Figuring that we could arrive in time to avoid the bad weather, we left as planned. Unfortunately for us, the storm arrived much earlier than we anticipated. At midnight, the sky lit up all along the horizon with lightning and the rain hit us horizontally with 35 miles-per-hour winds. Even though it was night, the lightning lit up the sky around us. There was so much electricity in the air that it seemed it was lighter more often than dark. The noise of the wind blowing through the rigging was beyond belief. It sounded like a freight train was running us over. We were too far offshore to seek shelter and could not turn back. The storm was ours. We had no choice but to test the strength of our boats and the spirit of its sailors.

This storm was one of the most memorable experiences of my sailing life. Not because of any tragedy. But, because of how proud I was of how well we dealt with it. We donned foul weather gear, lashed everything down that was loose, and remained calm throughout. Mark and I stayed below and let the autopilot steer us through the howling wind and seas. I kept an eye on the black seas ahead and watched our buddy boat through the starboard side porthole. Nothing broke. We did not suffer a knockdown. None of the lightning bolts struck our mast. The boat held up beautifully and the next morning we tied up to the city dock ready for a Bloody Mary and a nap.

Our friend had a completely different experience on his sailboat. They were sick and wet. One crewmember was so frightened, he thought that he would die. He counted his rosary beads while puking over the side. He swore never to go on a sailboat again. We were two similar boats, in the same body of water, in the same storm, but, with a completely different story to tell. Ours was one of pride at having fought a powerful storm at sea and triumphed. They told a story of terror, panic, and dread. Nothing bad happened on either boat. Everyone arrived safely. Yet, you would not know this if you were on the dock that morning.

My sailing story illustrates how dealing with unpleasantness is all about attitude. Attitude is a choice. It is a decision to calmly make the right decisions and trust that your decisions are correct. I also had to trust my boat and equipment and have faith that all the years of sailing experience that I had enjoyed would come in handy if anything failed. I never panicked and made sure that Mark had complete confidence in me so that he would not panic, either.

It is this same philosophy that guided me during those months before surgery. I knew that I was caught in a storm of disease. But, I had complete confidence that I was making the correct decision. For me, surgery was the right choice. For me, Dr. Su was the right man to cure me. For me, I had nothing to fear now that I had a clear direction and plan. I knew that I would easily survive this storm and that, in the end, I would have a good yarn to share.

So, as I said earlier, the months between my decision to have surgery and the surgery date were some of the best of my life. A friend told me that it might help to develop my core so that I would recover faster from the procedure.

My wife encouraged me to hire a personal trainer, which I did. For the first time in my life I worked out with weights on a regular basis. I was determined to be physically fit when I arrived for surgery. I would strongly encourage anyone having time to prepare for surgery to do the same. I am not certain that there is research to show to that it helps, but it certainly did help me emotionally. I felt that I had some control over the outcome of the procedure. I also felt good physically.

I had fun with my condition. I told my wife that she was obligated to have sex with me whenever I wanted. After all, I had cancer and might become impotent. We laughed about this often and had lots of sex. Whenever Judy was annoyed with me about anything, I said, "don't pick on me, I have cancer." It became a running joke that I did not have to wash the dishes because I had cancer.

One potential complication from prostate surgery is incontinence. I read that after surgery, the Kegel muscles are the primary way to hold urine. These muscles located on the pelvic floor are used when a man attempts to stop urine flow while urinating. A great exercise to strengthen the Kegel muscles is to practice discontinuing urination in mid-flow. I did this exercise regularly when urinating and got good at it. I am confident that strengthening these muscles before surgery helped my recovery, though I have no clue whether there is scientific evidence to prove this.

I told my partner at our law practice that I had to take a month off from work because I was having my penis cut off. I reveled in the attention that I got from my condition. People told me how sorry they were to hear about my diagnosis, and I laughed and talked about my sex life. Because of the decision that I made, I felt (and still do) certain that I would not die of prostate cancer. Though, for the next 4 months, I would have the best time of my life. I laughed more than ever. I did not lose a moment of sleep worrying about work. I sailed and spent time with my family. I did not worry for a moment about what would happen. It was all Dr. Su's problem now and was completely off my shoulders.

Speaking of taking a month off from work, I was amazed at how, throughout my entire career, I never took longer than a 2-week vacation. I always felt that my law practice could not survive without my presence in the office. I dreamed of someday taking an extended vacation and perhaps sailing through the Caribbean. But, that would be impossible until I retired. However, when I needed to clear a month on my calendar to recover from surgery, I had no difficulty at all. I came to the realization that we set up pointless arbitrary limits to realizing our dreams. Of course the world could survive with me taking an extended vacation. I needed to get cancer to realize this.

So, my advice for preparation for prostate surgery is simple: 1) have lots of sex, 2) take a vacation and enjoy life, 3) exercise with a personal trainer and build your core, 4) diet if you are overweight, 5) clear your work calendar for a month following the surgery, and 6) laugh a lot.

Chapter Seven

Surgery

The day prior to surgery, I needed to go to Gainesville for preparation. It was a busy day, with visits to the surgeon and pre-op screening. The screening included an EKG. I happen to have a hairy chest and had fun by shaving myself completely a few weeks prior to the surgery. The nurse administering my EKG laughed and thanked me for making her job easier as she removed the wires from my shaved chest. I also submitted to a chest X-ray, blood tests and, once again, the obligatory urine test.

Part of my surgery preparation involved thinking about how I would feel after the surgery. It occurred to me that I would be in a car driving 2 ½ hours the day after surgery. I worried about whether I would feel every bump in the road. In anticipation of this, I brought a pillow and blanket in the car to make things more comfortable. I also thought about what kind of clothing I might need. I had been told that I would be going home with a catheter. Considering the location of the incisions near my belly button, I figured that I should wear very loose clothing. I bought large sweat pants and figured the catheter bag might fit in the pants and the waist would be loose enough to be comfortable. I had never worn sweat pants regularly, but they would be the only pants I would wear for the next six weeks.

I do not recall now whether I was nervous about the events of the following day. I do recall being busy running from one appointment to the next. My diet that day was limited so that I would have an empty stomach in the morning. I was permitted a light breakfast with just fluids for the remainder of the day and nothing after midnight. I do recall that prior to going to sleep at our hotel, I had to take a shower and wash myself with a special soap known as Chlorhexidine so that I would be extra clean in order to prevent infection both the night before and morning of surgery. I missed my happy hour cocktail which had become a part of my routine over the prior months, and went to sleep with my alarm set for an early morning wake-up call.

I had to wake at 6 a.m. to give myself a fleet enema, followed by the short drive to the hospital. I remember sitting in the waiting room for no more than five minutes before being called back for surgery. As I lay in a hospital bed in a gown, I was approached by several residents and interns who said they would be assisting with the surgery. They all assured me that I had one of the best surgeons in the country and they were ready to get to work. I must have been asked 10 times what type of surgery I was there for and had a different answer each time. I was either having a hair transplant (I am completely bald) or a penis reduction. Each time I got a good laugh out of the staff. Finally, I kissed my wife and was rolled into the operating room. Dr. Su met me there and said hello as I was being transferred to the table and prepared. I recall seeing the wires and machines that make up the robotic tools used for the procedure. The room seemed to be full of people each busy performing some task to prepare for what would happen. There seemed to be a large crowd there just for me. I asked Dr. Su if he had had a good night's sleep and whether he was feeling lucky. He smiled. The last thing I remember before dozing off was seeing the clock on the wall, which read 8:15.

I awoke in recovery and noticed the clock said 3:30. I could not believe it. Why had I been asleep for so long? Was there a complication? Did everything go ok? I was surprised at how alert I felt. It was similar to the feeling of waking after a colonoscopy. I really felt rested and aware of my surroundings. I recall speaking to a nurse and an intern who both told me that everything had gone very well. There were no serious complications though the doctors did fix a hernia near my belly button. One that I did not know I had before the surgery. My wife, Judy, came in the recovery room and she sounded great. She told me that she had spoken to the surgeon and was told that everything went well and he felt that the cancer was contained in the prostate. He also told her that he felt he did a good job preserving the nerves. All looked good. I was told that the procedure took 4 hours of which time 45 minutes was related to repairing the hernia at my belly button and that this was not unusual nor should I read anything negative into this fact. The loss of time may have been related to my being anesthetized.

It was not long before the medical staff was ready to move me to my room outside of recovery. As an indication of how alert I was, I stopped the nurses as they rolled me out of recovery. I told them that my clothes had been taken by them while I was being prepped and put in a locker. I asked them to locate the bag of clothes for me. They had forgotten this and went to the locker, found my belongings, and placed them under the bed.

When I got to the hospital room, I was greeted by my wife, my boys, and my wife's best friend who had traveled to Gainesville to keep her company. She presented me with a huge chocolate penis. I remember taking it out in front of the nurses and staff in my room and we all had a big laugh. Shortly after this, a UF student came into my room and played a few songs on his guitar. I must say that I woke up feeling good physically. Being surrounded by a friendly hospital staff, my family and friends, and listening to beautiful music, made that moment in time one that I will always cherish. The worst was behind me.

I found it interesting that I had a bit of lower back pain and pain in my butt. The interns explained to me that this pain was from the pressure of laying on a surface without any movement for 4 hours. They had placed cushions under me before the surgery to try to prevent this from happening. But, they said that it does none the less. The pain did go away soon after the surgery. But, it is significant that this was my biggest complaint that night. Not the incisions, not the catheter, but relatively minor back pain.

Dr. Su gave me strict instructions to walk. He told me that I needed to walk twice around the floor of the hospital before midnight and at least a city block six times per day after returning home. I understood that the purpose of the walking was to prevent against blood clot formation, encourage a speedy recovery, and to encourage bowels to begin functioning once again. Apparently constipation is a common side effect of being sedated for a long period of time. Dr. Su warned me not to eat too much too soon since it would take time for my digestive system to begin functioning again.

That evening, I got out of bed twice and walked the floor with my IV stand and Foley catheter. I do not recall feeling much pain that evening. I had never had a catheter before and it was a bit clumsy and uncomfortable. I was warned by a nurse who saw me walk to be very careful not to step on the long catheter tube or "all kinds of hell will break loose." After prostate removal, the urethra is re-attached to the base of the bladder. The catheter keeps the connection open as the surgical connection heals. I would have to have the catheter in place for at least a week after surgery.

That night I did not reject offers of pain pills. Frankly, the pills were more for discomfort than pain. I do not recall sleeping at all, though I likely nodded off for brief spells. Even if I was able to sleep, I doubt the nurses would have allowed it. They came in regularly to take blood pressure and change my catheter. I wondered how I would manage that myself. Little did I know that I would soon become an expert.

The morning after surgery, Dr. Su offered to discharge me. I saw no reason to remain in the hospital and by 10 a.m. I was in my wheelchair on the sidewalk outside waiting for my wife to bring up the car. Nineteen hours after leaving the recovery room I was on my way home.

Chapter Eight

Recovery

The hospital sent me home with two catheter bags and instructions on how to change, use, and clean the whole contraption. One bag was small and able to be strapped to my leg. The other, much larger bag, could be hung anywhere lower than my bladder. I used the small bag for the drive home, but used it rarely after that. I found it much more convenient to use the larger bag which could be emptied less frequently, and without having to take off my pants. I cut a small incision in a pocket of my sweatpants and ran the tube through the hole in the pocket. That way the tube could bend comfortably in the pocket and outside my sweatpants. When sitting at home, I would pull a kitchen chair nearby and hang the catheter on a cross bar under the chair.

During my six-time-a-day walks, I would usually carry my catheter bag with a towel draped over my arm to hide it. I experienced no pain or discomfort during these walks, though it was a chore. It did force me off the couch regularly and, I am sure, helped speed the recovery. The catheter itself was somewhat uncomfortable and the pain pills usually helped with that. Sleeping was a little more challenging because I could not safely roll over without carefully holding the tube to make sure it did not get yanked.

I had been warned that it would be uncomfortable having the catheter for so long. Occasionally the tip of my penis felt irritated or I would get sharp pains in that area. When that happened, I took a Percocet which seemed to make the irritation less noticeable. It was important to clean the area around the tip of the penis so that the fluid near the tip would not dry and stick to the tube.

I worried somewhat about my ability to hold urine once the catheter was removed. I often tested my Kegel muscles to see if they responded which they did. I wonder whether those who have the catheter for longer periods than me have more continence issues. I wanted mine out as soon as possible. In fact, I scheduled a return trip to Gainesville to have the catheter removed by a different surgeon before mine returned from a conference. I did not want to wear this for an extra three days if it was not absolutely necessary.

Removing the catheter is not a painful experience. The doctor injects a fluid into the catheter tube while watching the bladder on a screen to see if there is any leakage. Once it is confirmed that the connection has healed, the doctor quickly releases the balloon on the end of the catheter in the bladder and pulls it out. It takes a moment, and there is no pain or discomfort. I was absolutely thrilled when the doctor asked me to urinate into a pan and stop the flow. It worked! I was able to have urinary control.

After removal of the catheter I was given an adult "pull up" type diaper to wear. I had my wife stop two or three times on the way home so that I could visit the bathroom. The diaper was dry when I got home.My two boys had bought me an Apple TV as a gift over the holidays knowing that I would be watching a lot during my recovery. This device allowed me to watch movies and programs streamed over the Internet on my TV. I have to say that the weeks following my surgery were quite relaxing and I felt a bit guilty about behaving so lazily. The doctors told me that I would not be returning to work for about a month. But honestly, I felt that once the catheter was removed and I was off pain pills, I could return immediately. As a lawyer, my job generally involves sitting at a desk and staring at a computer screen. This was physically not much different from what I was doing at home on my couch in front of a large TV.

One big annoyance during the days after surgery related to difficulty moving my bowels. I was clearly constipated and had been warned not to strain while on the toilet. I found that when I did strain, there was some blood that dripped from the penis. This was disconcerting, but I was assured by the surgeon's nurse that it was normal. But, by taking a stool softener, drinking water constantly, and walking, things eventually started to function properly.

Eight days after the surgery I had the catheter removed, I was off Percocet and I felt ready to return to the office. I was in the office 10 days after surgery. My wife forbade me from working full days. At first I worked three hours per day. Three weeks post-surgery, I was back to a full-time schedule. I did continue to wear my sweat pants for a few weeks after surgery so that there would not be pressure on the surgical incisions on the belt line.

I was advised not to return to vigorous exercise for at least four weeks. These instructions were amended to five weeks because they repaired a hernia during my surgery. By five weeks I was completely pain-free as if I had never had the procedure, and was ready to run and lift weights.

Chapter Nine

Return to Continence and Potency

While researching treatment options, I was a little frustrated by my difficulty in getting specific detailed information about what to expect after surgery. Many people answered in generalities while I wanted specifics. Some men answered my questions with humor and others barely at all. Even my doctor, who wanted to give me detailed answers, was non-committal when it came to specifics. So, if you want specifics, I will share them with you.

Before you continue with this chapter be forewarned. If you were ever at a party and you told someone that what they just said was "TMI," skip this chapter. If you are easily offended or embarrassed, skip this chapter. If you are my mother, mother-in-law, or one of my children or their girlfriends, skip this chapter. If you work with me, skip this chapter.

In fact, if you are a friend of mine on Facebook, you may as well skip this chapter.

I plan to tell you exactly how my life has been affected by prostate surgery with as much detail as I can. I am doing this because I believe that it will be very useful in helping others decide whether surgery is right for them. I am going to tell you about particulars that I was afraid to ask others and no one offered to share. By doing this, I am risking the possibility that I will offend others and embarrass myself. But I believe that if sharing will help others make the right choice for themselves, it is worth the risk of embarrassment.

I am certain that if you have surgery, your results will be different from mine. Just as our bodies did not perform identically before surgery, I am certain they will perform differently afterwards. Also, no doctor worth his salt will guarantee any return or level of return of potency or continence. So, take what you read with a grain of salt. Be assured that your experience will certainly be better, or worse, than mine.

When a man chooses surgery while still having an active sex life, he is normally mainly concerned about losing his ability to have an erection strong enough for sexual intercourse. This was the way I felt and what worried me the most about choosing surgery. This fear was foolish in the sense that it should not be nearly as big a concern as losing the ability to control one's urine. If you live long enough, you may end up outliving your sex drive. But, you will urinate until the day you die.

Potty Training After Surgery

So even though urinary control may not be your biggest concern, I will start with it because it should be your most important concern. I was blessed because I was able to stop my urine flow the moment the catheter was removed. After removal, I wore an adult disposable brief for a few days and at night for a few months.

For the first few months, I wore a depends guard or shield in my underwear. I found this to be much more comfortable than the bulky briefs. Also, I found that if I went to the bathroom often, the guard stayed dry. During the first few months, they only needed to be changed out 2 or 3 times per day.

As was discussed earlier, the mechanics of holding urine is significantly different post-surgery. Instead of three muscle groups holding urine, there is now only one. Before surgery, urine was controlled by a muscle at the base of the bladder, the prostate, and the Kegel muscles at the pelvic floor. After surgery, you only have your Kegel muscles to control your urine. I wondered how that would feel. Since the Kegel muscles tire easily when you exercise, I had wondered if they would be tense and painful 24 hours a day. The answer is no. You can be totally relaxed and not urinate unless your bladder is full. In that case, you must clench your muscles to prevent leakage.

Shortly after surgery, I sensed that when I went to the bathroom to urinate, the urine flow started much sooner than before. It seemed to flow instantly when I was ready. Now that I am over a year post-surgery, I no longer notice any difference in the way I urinate.

After surgery, I made it a point to go to the toilet the moment I sensed I had to go. I found myself using the bathroom twice as often as before surgery. Now I no longer feel that I urinate any more often than most of the healthy women who work in my office. I may not have a bladder of steel, but it does not impair me in any way.

I never, even immediately after surgery, had a complete loss of urine while I was awake. I would have some leakage at times. If I felt that I had to urinate, sometimes a little urine would leak in the instant before I clenched the Kegel muscles. After about 4-5 months post-surgery, I no longer needed to wear a guard during the day. I no longer have leakage while awake except for those rare times when I have had way too much alcohol to drink. While awake, I feel that there is now very little difference in urinary control before and after surgery.

Sleeping after prostate surgery is a different issue altogether. I found it very uncomfortable to sleep with disposable briefs because they were bulky and hot. Sometimes when I woke up, I was not certain whether the moisture in the briefs was urine or sweat. After about three months, I began sleeping with guards in my underwear. I found this much more comfortable, but not as effective in preventing leakage into the bed. As extra protection, I always, even to this day, sleep with an extra pad under the sheets.

Controlling urine flow after surgery is a more conscious control issue than it was before surgery. Therefore, when sleeping, you are far more likely to urinate in bed especially if you are sleeping heavily or had consumed alcohol in the evening.

Six months after surgery, I found that I could sleep without a guard and had very few nighttime accidents. Today I still occasionally urinate in bed. It is very unusual and probably happens about one time every few months. It seems to be rarer as time goes on. When it does happen, I blame myself. Sometimes I am awakened in the middle of the night by an urge to urinate. But, rather than force myself awake and to the bathroom, I fall back to sleep before getting out of bed. Sometimes I simply drink too many fluids late at night, or too much wine. This urinary control issue is so minor and so rare, that I have not let it change the way I live my life. If I want a drink at night, I have it. But, I am careful to use the extra bed pad and take a small one with me when I sleep away from home.

Generally speaking, I feel that my urinary control is now completely normal. I suspect that many healthy men and woman have the same control issues as I have now. I have heard that it is far more difficult to regain urinary control when you have the surgery at a later age. But, if you are in your 50s or are a physically active older man, you may be able to enjoy the same experience I have had. If you do not, I understand that there are Kegel muscle exercises that can be done to improve control as well as physical therapy.

Everything You Wanted to Know About Sex, but Were Afraid to Ask

Whether you can obtain an erection after surgery depends on a multitude of factors including your age, your preoperative erectile function, having an active sexual partner, and whether your surgeon was able to preserve the nerves surrounding the prostate. It was explained to me that these nerves are so tiny that they are not visible to the doctor. Instead, he or she works to protect the thin membrane containing the nerves. They are almost assuredly assaulted during the procedure and do take time to recover.

My surgeon had explained to me that my sexual function might return, but it would take time for the nerves to recover and would never be quite as good as before. He told me that patients my age who are preoperatively potent and have their nerves preserved have an approximately 70% chance of reporting successful intercourse at 6 months and 85% at one year, but that most are not at 100% of the baseline. I thanked him for that explanation, but still had no clue what it meant. Would this mean that I would want to have sex as often as before? Did it mean that my erection would be less strong then before the surgery? Other than knowing I would have a good chance of having intercourse again, what should I expect sex to be like?

I ran into a friend at a party before my surgery who had his prostate removed several years earlier. I asked him about his sex life. He laughed and told me to pull his finger. I laughed, but was still totally perplexed. What did that joke have to do with his sex life? I called another man my age who had had the same procedure that I was having. He told me quite seriously that after surgery, he had a talk with his wife and now his sex life was fine. I thanked him, but really wanted to know what he told his wife and what his wife is doing now and especially what he meant when he said that his sex life was fine.

So, do you want to know how surgery has affected my sex life? Pull my finger!

Just joking. Of course I will tell you. The prior paragraphs were just my stall technique. No man wants to talk about it, but every man wants to know.

The day I returned home from the doctor without a catheter, I was dying to know if I still had life in my penis. Sex was still out of the question since my wounds were still fresh. So, I waited for my wife to fall asleep and left the room to gently masturbate. With some additional blood flowing, but not really what could be considered an erection, I experienced a very satisfying orgasm. In fact, it was tremendous since my fears were alleviated and I knew that my sex life was not over.

My surgeon prescribed Viagra and Cialis to assist with erections. He told me to take once a day, low dose Cialis, for several months after surgery to improve blood flow and preserve the penile tissues based upon basic science research studies. He indicated that this would not, however, make the nerves recover faster. I did take the Cialis for a few weeks, but noticed nothing. No spontaneous erections and no stronger erections when I was trying.

After enough time had passed that I was cleared for physical activity, about 5 weeks post-surgery, I was able to attempt sex. However, I could not yet sustain a strong enough erection for sexual intercourse.

I spoke to Dr. Su, and he recommended that I purchase a vacuum external penile pump and use that in conjunction with Cialis. The penile pump consists of a plastic tube that fits over your penis and either uses a hand pump or battery powered electric pump, to draw the air out of the tube which draws blood into the penis. After obtaining a sufficient erection, a tight rubber ring is slipped off of the tube onto the base of the penis. The vacuum in the tube is released and the tube removed. The purpose of the rubber ring is to prevent too much blood from exiting the penis so that it can remain erect throughout intercourse. Interestingly, the pump is considered to be a medical device and was partially paid for by my insurance.

The pump worked adequately for me for a period of time after I got up the operational learning curve. My experience indicates that the pump is not really effective without some sexual stimulation. Therefore, my wife and I would start with some sexual foreplay followed by me running to the bathroom and beginning the process of assembling the pump.

It helps to be somewhat mechanically inclined to assemble the pump before the mood escapes. First, the tube is inserted on the pump. Next, you must spread lubricant on a cone shaped object as well as around, on, and into the tube. The cone is then placed on the tube. The stiff rubber ring is placed on an "injector" and pushed around the cone until it is spread wide enough to fit on the end of the tube. Once the rubber ring is on the tube, the cone is removed and a rubber gasket type ring is placed on the open end of the tube to allow for the creation of a vacuum between the tube and your skin. Now you are ready to pump!

You place the tube over your penis and against your skin. CAREFULLY, pump the air out of the tube stopping ever few seconds to allow blood to be drawn into the penis. I found that it was quite painful if you pumped too quickly. I also found that it helps to release the vacuum and allow a very small amount of air into the tube every 10 seconds or so and then pump again.

After about a minute of pumping, releasing a bit, and pumping some more, I found that I had a pretty strong erection. At that point, I released a slight amount of air into the tube (not too much, but just enough so that my penis was not in pain), and then slipped the stiff rubber ring off the tube onto the base of my penis. I could then release the pressure completely and join my patient wife in the bedroom.

One would think that the tiny stiff rubber ring could harm your penis by cutting off blood circulation. It can! The manual does warn not to leave it on for extended lovemaking (my words). During sex, the ring did not cause any pain. However, it always hurt a bit to remove the ring when finished, especially when pulled over the tip of the penis.

The use of the vacuum pump with Cialis made for a very satisfying sex life. When I first began using the pump, the thought was that it would only be needed for a limited amount of time while the surgically stressed nerves healed.

According to Dr. Su, it is normal for men to have multiple erections while they sleep. In fact, there is risk that if the nerves are so damaged that these nocturnal erections do not occur, the muscles can, in effect, atrophy and be permanently damaged. The pump manual itself encourages the user to exercise these muscles daily by using the pump every morning to create an erection. I tried to pump a day or two each week, but found it to be annoying and time consuming. Unfortunately, as the months went by, I never found much of an improvement in penile function. I continued to be dependent upon the pump for an erection and rarely noticed a nocturnal erection, if at all.

After about a year of using the pump, I scheduled an appointment with Dr. Su and drove back to Gainesville. I was ready to try a different option. Frankly, I wanted to find out if there would be a way to avoid having to rely on this device for the rest of my sexual life.

The next option Dr. Su recommended was the Trimix penile injection therapy. Finally, we are getting to the good stuff. Trimix is a mixture of three drugs injected directly into the penis. Dr. Su explained that this drug is very effective and can even lead to improvement of sexual function after regular use. He said that there are two primary reasons why it is not prescribed before trying the pump. First, many men have an aversion to sticking a needle in their penis. Ok, I get that!! Secondly, there is a greater risk of developing priapism with Trimix. Priapism is the medical term for erections that last too long and may require medical attention. He said that if I were interested, I would need to first order and receive the prescription for the Trimix and return to his office for a training session on how to inject it. The plan was for me to return with the drug and actually have an erection in the doctor's office. I was ready to give it try.

Trimix is made by a compound pharmacy and must be refrigerated. Although it is not covered by my insurance, I found it to be reasonably priced as compared to Viagra or Cialis. It was difficult to know how much to order at first because the drug only lasts about 90 days in the refrigerator. The quantity of Trimix depends upon the person. To prevent priapism, I would be starting with a small quantity injection which could be increased if needed. I booked an appointment to return to Gainesville and see a physician's assistant who would train me on using my new drug. I ordered the prescription which arrived with 10 needles and alcohol swabs.

When the day arrived, I invited my wife to join me but she politely declined. I joked that I would need help with my penis, but she was not persuaded. It turned out to be a very unusual and interesting day. When I arrived at the doctor's office, I was sent to a typical exam room where a very professional female PA asked me to take off my pants so that she could show me how to inject the Trimix. For the first time since a college fraternity hazing episode, my penis was placed next to a tape measure and the length and circumference were duly noted in my permanent medical records. The PA demonstrated how to clean the surface of my penis with alcohol and draw the drug out of the bottle with the needle. She showed how to select injection spots on the side of the penis and inject. Next, she advised me to massage my penis to encourage the drug to spread into the muscle.

Just in case you were not paying attention to the prior paragraph, let me review what happened one more time. A young attractive woman, who I was not married to, had me undress, handled my penis, measured it, gave me an erection, and then instructed me to masturbate. Well, not quite. The experience was completely professional and appropriate.

But it struck me at the time that I had a fantastic story to tell my friends.

The PA told me that she would return in about 10 minutes and handed me an office gown to place over my penis in case someone walked in on me. The effect of the drug was fast and remarkable. Within minutes I had an erection that was as strong as any I could recall at any stage of my life. The PA returned to the room, pulled the gown off my penis, and took out the tape measure again diligently noting them in her chart. I asked what she wrote down and she replied in centimeters. She asked me how this erection compared to when I was 18 and I told her that I did not see any difference. As she left again, she said that she would be back in 20 minutes. In case you were wondering what happened during those 20 minutes, I will tell you that the first thing I did was reach for my cell phone and googled how to convert centimeters to inches.

When the PA returned and noted that I still had an erection, she offered to inject another drug which would, like an antidote, return the penis to a flaccid state. I asked if I could simply wait longer for it to go down. I was interested in finding out if I would have priapism without the antidote. She told me I could stay as long as I wanted and agreed not to inject the drug. An hour later, I felt as though my erection had softened to the point where I could put on my blue jeans and I left the office to meet my son for dinner.

A funny thing happened as I left dinner and was about to head home. As I was about to pull onto the interstate for the two-hour drive home, I realized that I still had an erection though 3 hours had passed since my injection. I pulled into a gas station concerned that once I got on the interstate, I might not be near a hospital for at least two more hours. Would I be permanently injured for having an erection that lasted so long? I called the after-hours emergency number to speak to an on-call doctor at the medical clinic. After a few minutes of waiting, the doctor explained that as long as my erection was not painful and my penis was not turning blue or cold to the touch, there was still adequate blood circulation and I should not be worried. I headed onto the highway and, before too long, I was comfortable again.

At first, the Trimix caused me to have an erection for hours at a time to the point of being uncomfortable. An orgasm did not weaken the erection. I tried using a smaller dosage but found that any smaller dosage in the syringe did not work. The doctor prescribed a weaker dose which seems to have solved this problem. The only major drawback I found to using Trimix is that the erection will last at least an hour. This makes quickies or morning sex inconvenient.

I found that injecting the needle in the penis was not particularly painful. The benefits of using Trimix far outweighed this small amount of discomfort. You can use Trimix before beginning foreplay and it works like a charm all the time so long as you use the correct dosage. I found that it is far easier and more comfortable than the vacuum pump. In retrospect, I wish that I had skipped the vacuum pump phase completely and gone straight to Trimix.

After about six months of using Trimix, I noticed that I was having nocturnal erections again as well as solid erections with just Viagra or Cialis and no Trimix. I foresee stopping Trimix eventually and just using the pills. I cannot be certain that the Trimix solved my erectile dysfunction issues. It is possible that it may have resolved itself with time. But, I am inclined to believe that after a year of the pump, the Trimix helped my penile muscles and awakened the nerves.

The orgasm is certainly different after the removal of the prostate. First of all, it is a dry orgasm. There is no ejaculate. But, the orgasm originates in the brain and it is most definitely still there even without an ejaculation. According to Dr. Su, some men report that the orgasm takes much longer to occur and is somewhat less intense. My sense is that the orgasm is far more complicated than it used to be. I imagine it is more like a female orgasm in the sense that it is a bit more difficult to reach and depends entirely on your mental state. Sometimes it is subtle and other times intense.

Before my prostate was removed, there was no question when the orgasm occurred. There was physical proof. Now it is occasionally intense and, at other times, barely noticeable if it happens at all. I do feel that I enjoy sex as much as I always did. But, like many women (I suspect), sex is not always focused on achieving orgasm. I understand why some women "fake" an orgasm after a lengthy period of pleasurable sex.

I cannot add much to this except to say that I do not miss the way it used to be. I continue to have sex and continue to gain pleasure from it.

My sex drive is as strong as it was before my surgery. It is easier now to achieve an erection in that the Trimix leaves no room for performance anxiety or other factors that might interfere.

Chapter Ten

Breaking Bad

While recovering from my surgery, I forced myself the guilty pleasure of binge TV watching. During the evening, my wife and I went on a streak watching the entire 62 episodes of Breaking Bad, sometimes several shows a night. In case you do not know, Breaking Bad is an extremely entertaining fictional crime drama about Walter White, a 50-year-old high school chemistry teacher diagnosed with lung cancer. In an effort to secure the financial future of his family, he decides to use his chemistry skills to "cook" crystal meth. He secures the aid of a former student, Jesse Pinkman, to be his partner in the enterprise.

As one would expect, the business spirals out of control and before long, Walter's life and family are in grave and constant danger. Walter must resort to deception and murder to protect them and everything he has. What makes the series particularly intriguing is that Walter's brother-in-law, Hank, is a DEA agent who is tasked with fighting the crystal meth empire in their community. Hank never imagines that his sick, wimpish, high school teacher brother-in-law could possibly be the man responsible for flooding the streets with the most potent crystal meth they had ever seen.

What Hank and the others in the family failed to see was the change that the cancer diagnosis had in Walt. In one episode, Walt explained that since he was diagnosed with cancer, he was no longer afraid of anything. Having lived most of his life with fear of risk and regrets for failing to take risk, he was now willing to break the law and deal with the most dangerous elements in society. Walt had changed to a different person and no one but Walt knew who that person was.

Watching Walter on television, I related to this change. Before meeting with Dr. Su, I worried constantly about whatever there was to worry about. Most of all, I worried about my law practice and whether we would generate the income needed to make payroll. I worried about whether I would have the money to pay my mortgage and continue enjoying what I could afford. This worry would often keep me up at night.

After meeting with Dr. Su for our initial consultation, the fear and feelings of dread suddenly dissipated. A huge weight unexpectedly lifted off my shoulders. Of course, I cared about the firm's finances, but I did not have room for the anxiety and apprehension about matters that now seemed trivial. I felt happier and less stressed than I had felt in years. On the night I returned from Gainesville following my first appointment, I fell asleep the moment my head hit the pillow.

There is nothing like cancer to make one realize what is really important in life and how to organize one's priorities. For my entire working career, I had never taken more than a 2-week vacation. I fantasized about taking off for an entire month or two in order to enjoy a long cruise in my sailboat. But I knew that I could never do it because of the demands in my practice. Once I realized that I needed to clear an entire month to recover from cancer surgery, I had no problem whatsoever. Why was it that I could clear my calendar for surgery, but in 34 years of practice, could never do it for a vacation?

Once I let go of my fear and anxiety, I began to smile more. Having this diagnosis actually enhanced my enjoyment of life. I used my sense of humor to deal with most of the daily stresses of life. When my wife got annoyed with me about something, I would look at her and say, "is that any way to talk to a man with cancer?" She would break out laughing and it became a running joke.

Before my surgery, I decided I would use this diagnosis to my advantage. My wife could not turn down my sexual advances. After all, I might soon be impotent! When my friend asked me to join him for a "guys weekend" away, what could Judy say except for, "go ahead and enjoy"? I joked to my friends that I needed to have some fun because I was about to have surgery to have my dick cut off.

I suddenly was able to enjoy life to its fullest, shedding the weight of fear and anxiety. Unlike Walter White, I did not see the need to live a life of crime. But, by removing fear, I was able to enjoy life so much more.

I am proud of how I responded to my diagnosis. Not everyone would see it the way I did. But, I can say without hesitation, that the way I responded is the best. I thought about my options, I did my research, and I consulted with my wife, experts, and friends. It took me about 3 weeks to decide on surgery and I forged ahead with plans. Most importantly, I made up my mind to enjoy every day to its fullest. To exercise, eat well, kiss my wife, and have sex as often as possible. The time between my diagnosis and my surgery was one of the most pleasant worry-free times in my life.

By the way, even though I stopped obsessing about firm finances, the firm still exists, and we have not missed a payroll. The worry, fretfulness, and anxiety accomplished nothing except to disrupt my sleep. I think I needed to have cancer to learn this valuable lesson. The only things that really matter are love, health, family, and friends.

As I put the finishes touches on this book, I am now over two years post-surgery. I am almost entirely continent and enjoy a wonderful sex life. Best of all, I am cancer free. I feel as though I am less stressed than I used to be and look back on my diagnosis, surgery, and recovery as a wonderful life adventure. I hope that as you read this book, you feel less stress about your diagnosis and make your treatment decisions based on objective facts and not out of fear. I am witness to how surgery, performed by the right doctor, can lead to a wonderful outcome. I hope this helps you make the right decision for you.

Good luck!!

Several months after my surgery, I had the opportunity to tour the Operating Room and view and photograph the equipment used for my surgery at Shands Hospital at the University of Florida in Gainesville. My surgeon used the Da Vinci surgical system.

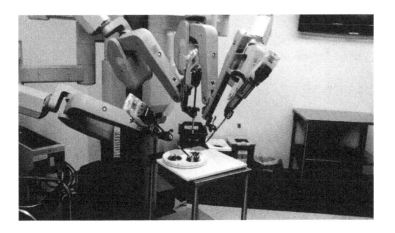

These are the probes inserted through small incisions in the abdomen which are the tools used to perform the procedure.

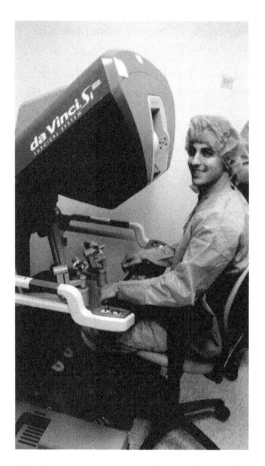

This is my son, Jacob Ludin, sitting at the controls. The toggles in front of his hands control the probes shown in the earlier photograph. At the time of publication of this book, Jacob was a medical student at the University of Florida. The surgeon's back is to the patient as he watches the probes using the monitor in front of Jacob's head.

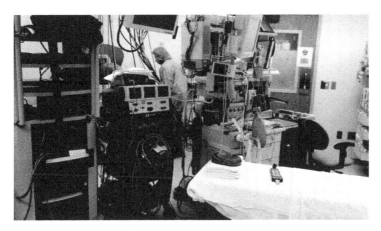

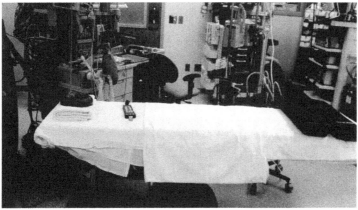

The network of wires and equipment operated by the many
assistants during surgery.

My remarkable surgeon: Dr. Li-Ming Su, M.D.

Dr. Su is now the Chairman of the Department of Urology at the University of Florida College of Medicine.

Made in United States
Orlando, FL
26 November 2021